Helen Keller

written and illustrated
by Jessica Clerk

McGraw-Hill
School Division

New York   Farmington

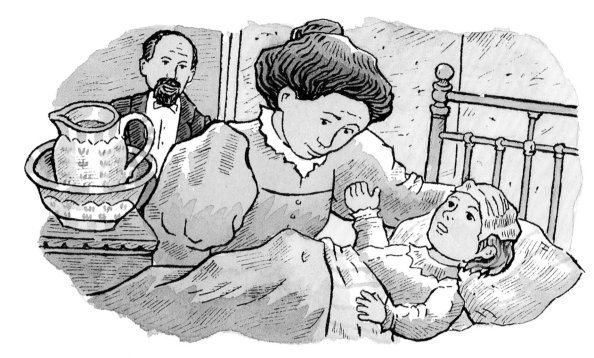

No one knew for certain the name of the disease that baby Helen Keller had. "Acute congestion of the stomach and brain," the family doctor had said. He doubted that she would survive.

As the child burned with fever, her mother nursed her day and night, cooling her forehead, soothing her as best she could. At last, the fever abated, and as far as anyone could tell, Helen had recovered. Yet although Helen had survived, she would never be the same. The unknown illness had left her blind and deaf.

Helen Keller was born on June 27, 1880, in Tuscumbia, Alabama. She was the child of Captain Arthur Keller, and his wife, Kate Adams Keller. Helen had been a lively, happy little girl. At six months she could nearly talk, and she started walking before her first birthday. After she was stricken at nineteen months old, everything changed.

The lively child became dull and unresponsive. Because she could not hear, she could not learn to speak. Now Helen explored her world by clinging fearfully to her mother's skirts. Yet despite the great changes she endured, her intelligence and spirit survived. Later, she described this time in her life: "My hands felt every object and observed every motion, and in this way I learned to know many things."

As she got older, she found ways to communicate with people, acting out to get what she wanted. Did she want ice cream? Shivering with cold, she pretended to turn the handle on the ice-cream freezer. If she wanted bread and butter, Helen mimed cutting a slice of bread and spreading it with butter. She had signs to indicate her mother and father; in fact she devised over sixty signs in all.

Helen could learn simple tasks: "I understood a great deal of what was going on around me. At five I learned to fold and put away the clean clothes when they were brought in from the laundry, and I distinguished my own from the rest." Somehow Helen always understood when her mother wanted her to bring her something.

It was not enough, though; her world was still a baffling and chaotic place, and she had no key to how to make sense of it.

The older she grew, the more frustrated she became. Her moods shifted like lightning from calm to furious anger. Unpredictably, she lashed out, kicking, screaming, breaking lamps, dishes, whatever was in reach, until she had exhausted herself, and the storm passed.

The Kellers were not rich, and taking care of Helen was a tremendous strain. Members of the family argued constantly about what was to be done with her. Kate Keller's brother felt that Helen was mentally ill, and should be shut away; this was the standard treatment for many disabled people at the time. Helen's Auntie Ev, who adored her, sprang to her defense. "This child has more sense than all the Kellers," her Auntie Ev said, "if there is any way to reach her mind."

Kate, too, was certain that her child had intelligence, but how could she be taught? They lived far away from any school for blind or deaf people. Who would come to a remote place like Tuscumbia to teach a deaf-blind child?

In those days Kate Keller's only hope came from the English author, Charles Dickens. He had written an account of his visit to the United States, called *American Notes*. Dickens, the most famous writer in the world, was a social crusader, visiting poorhouses and hospitals, at home and abroad.

In Boston, he visited the Insane Asylum, the prison, and the Perkins Institution for the Blind. Vividly, he described his meeting with Laura Bridgman. Laura Bridgman was a deaf-blind child, like Helen, but Laura Bridgman *had been taught language!* Kate's hopes soared. If one child could be taught, why not Helen?

By now, Helen was less and less able to express her needs. The more she tried to communicate, the more frustrated she became; the tantrums and rages increased daily, sometimes hourly.

There was also a new problem. Kate Keller had had another child; now six-year-old Helen had to share her mother's attentions with a baby sister. Helen resented the strange creature who took up so much of her mother's time and affection. The last straw came one day when Helen discovered that the new baby and not her favorite doll was in the cradle. Furious, she overturned the cradle to pitch the intruder out. If Kate hadn't rushed to catch her, the baby might have been badly hurt.

Once again the relatives started in: "She is wild and out of control. She can be dangerous—Helen should be taken away."

That summer Kate and Arthur Keller brought Helen to Washington to meet with Dr. Alexander Graham Bell. This famous inventor of the telephone was also a teacher of the deaf, and an expert on schools for deaf and blind children.

Dr. Bell liked Helen immediately. "It's obvious that she's a bright child, a very teachable child." He advised Captain Keller to write to The Perkins Institution for the Blind and see if there was a teacher who could handle her education.

In a few weeks the director wrote back and told him that a teacher had been found. Her name was Anne Sullivan, and although she was only twenty-one, she had great strength of character.

Anne had been brought up in the poorhouse at Tewksbury, Massachusetts. She spent six years there, surrounded by poverty, dirt, and disease, gradually losing her sight to a chronic illness. At fourteen, she entered The Perkins Institution for the Blind. Although Anne knew less than the youngest child at her new school, she applied herself fiercely. She graduated with honors, the valedictorian of her class.

On March 3, 1887, Anne Sullivan arrived in Tuscumbia; it was to be the most important day in Helen's life.

For two days, the Kellers had gone to meet each train at the station. The house bustled with activity—Helen could tell that something was going to happen. She went outside and waited on the sunny porch.

Anne stepped down from the cart and approached the child. She ignored her tangled hair, and dirty dress, and reached for a kiss. Helen pushed her away, struggling, but soon her sensitive fingers explored the stranger's face, "seeing" it for the first time. Helen grabbed at Anne's bag, "which she insisted on opening at once, showing by signs that she expected to find something good to eat."

Soon after Anne arrived, the lessons began. The children at Perkins had sent Helen a doll; Anne unpacked it and gave it to Helen. After Helen had played with it a while, Anne reached for Helen's hand. Slowly, she spelled out the word "d-o-l-l." Helen was fascinated by the new game and tried to imitate it. At last she succeeded and ran downstairs to show her mother the new trick.

From then on, Anne spelled constantly in Helen's hand. With her intelligence and remarkable memory, Helen learned to spell many words in the days to come, particularly when she was rewarded by a piece of cake. But she was merely imitating Anne in the finger game. She had no idea that the words had any meaning.

Anne had spent the whole morning on just two words, trying to make Helen understand that m-u-g was mug and w-a-t-e-r was water. Again and again, she had spelled them into Helen's hand, but Helen kept confusing the words. At last, Anne led Helen outside.

"We walked down the path to the well-house.... Someone was drawing water and my teacher placed my hand under the spout. As the cool stream gushed over one hand she spelled into the other, the word water, first slowly, then rapidly. Somehow the mystery of language was revealed to me. I knew then that 'w-a-t-e-r' meant the wonderful cool something that was flowing over my hand."

For the first time Helen had a way to make sense of her world. *Things that could be named could be understood.* That day, Helen learned the words for mother, father, sister . . . and the word for teacher.

Helen learned with the speed of a locomotive. From the moment she woke up until she fell asleep, her appetite for words was insatiable. She grew to love Anne, the teacher and companion who had taught her to "speak."

Quickly, her mother and father began to study the manual alphabet and at last they could "talk" with their daughter! As the tantrums faded, Arthur and Kate Keller could barely recognize their little girl.

Anne soon stopped giving Helen formal lessons—she turned the whole outdoors into a classroom. On sunny days, they roamed into the countryside with a picnic basket, naming everything they came across. Helen asked questions about everything that slithered, flew, or crawled; about bugs, trees, bark, dirt, grass, flowers, ponds, puddles, tadpoles. If Helen picked an apple from a bushel, Anne explained about shapes. When she played with her dog's five new puppies, Anne showed her how to count.

In a flurry of letters to friends and to the director of the Perkins Institution, Anne Sullivan wrote about Helen's progress: "Helen is a wonderful child . . . Helen has learned about nine hundred words . . . Helen can read every word she can spell . . . ." Michael Anagnos, the director of Perkins, sent Anne teaching supplies that were especially designed for blind children.

By the middle of June, just three months after Anne arrived in Tuscumbia, Helen wrote her first letter. She'd learned to write block printing called "squarehand" by using a ruling board with grooves to guide the letters in. Helen could only keep track of her writing by concentrating hard, since the pencil left no mark, so Anne began to teach her Braille, the raised letters that blind people are taught to read and write.

At Perkins, there was growing excitement: Helen's progress was astounding; after just four months of teaching, *she had learned more than Laura Bridgman had in two years!*

Anagnos asked Anne to keep a careful record on her progress with Helen; in his annual report he published the record along with Helen's photograph and some of her letters. "Of all the blind and deaf-mute children," he wrote in 1888, "Helen Keller of Tuscumbia, Alabama, is undoubtedly the most remarkable." The report was read by many important and influential people in Boston. Anagnos sent copies to the newspapers too.

Overnight, Helen and Anne were famous! Journalists came knocking on the door of the Keller house in remote Tuscumbia, wanting to see this incredible child.

Now, the mailbox was overflowing with letters to Helen, sent by complete strangers, as well as by some of the most celebrated people of the time. Helen answered many of them, and began to correspond with people all over the country. Soon, she would write to people all over the world!

In June of 1888, Anne, Helen, and her family went to Boston. Helen attended the Perkins Institution for the Blind until the summer break. For the first time in her life, Helen was around children that were like her; children that could "talk" to her with the manual alphabet. Joyfully, she shared their studies and activities, and explored the school's raised maps and special typewriters. At last she had the luxury of a large library of books written in Braille.

During the summer, Helen and Anne stayed with friends in Cape Cod, and for the first time, Helen experienced the ocean. Fearless, she ran into the water, but she tripped on a rock and a wave knocked her down. "Who put salt in the water?" she asked as soon she was calm enough to spell.

In a few days she was back again, romping in the waves up to her ears. She explored the beach, looking for interesting shells. Extremely fond of animals, she tried to adopt a large horseshoe crab as a pet. By the end of that summer, the athletic little girl had learned to swim.

Everyone agreed that the visit to Perkins had been good for Helen, and in the fall of 1889, Anne accompanied her as she enrolled in the school. Soon after, Helen learned about Tommy Stringer, a child who was also deaf and blind. He had been sent to a hospital in Pennsylvania, and there was talk that he would end up in the poorhouse. Helen shuddered when she thought that Tommy might spend the rest of his life in grim isolation.

She decided to raise enough money for Tommy to come to Perkins. Helen wrote to her famous friends, asking for help for Tommy. She saved money herself by giving up her daily piece of candy. No one could resist her concern for others, and soon enough money had been raised to send Tommy to school for several years. For the first time, she was able to use her fame for the benefit of disabled people.

Everywhere they went, Helen and Anne were recognized and surrounded by people. In 1893, when they attended the Chicago World's Fair, Helen sparked nearly as much interest as the exhibits. The organizers of the fair allowed her to "see" all the exhibits with her sensitive fingers.

Eagerly, Helen examined African diamonds, bronze sculptures from France, gigantic guns from Germany—everything except the remains of Egyptian mummies!

Later, she wrote about the World's Fair in a letter that was published in *St. Nicholas*, one of the leading magazines for young people.

Yet writing and the manual alphabet were slow and clumsy ways to express her ideas. Helen wanted badly to be able to speak. When she heard that deaf-blind children had been taught to speak, she insisted on trying to learn, and spent two years at Wright-Humason School for the Deaf in New York. Although she worked terribly hard, many people had trouble understanding her speech. Fortunately, Anne was always at her side, to guide her and to interpret.

In New York, they met Mark Twain, the famous author of *Tom Sawyer* and *Huckleberry Finn*. Twain was dazzled by Helen's intelligence and sweetness, and they stayed friends for many years.

Despite her disabilities, Helen studied hard, determined to do as much as she could. She learned German, French, Latin, and Greek. English was always her favorite subject, and she showed promise as a writer. Her letters and poems were published in magazines like *St. Nicholas*, and the *Youth's Companion*. She began to think of writing as a career, but first, she decided to go to college.

Schools like Perkins and the Wright-Humason School for the Deaf were expensive, and Captain Keller was not rich. There was some concern that Helen's education might end. In 1896, friends like Alexander Graham Bell and Mark Twain started a trust to provide an annual income for Helen and Anne, as well as a scholarship for the rest of her education. Helen and Anne were deeply grateful. Helen would strive to make her friends proud of her.

On June 29, 1900, after two years of study, she sat
at her typewriter, preparing for the entrance exams at
Radcliffe College. Ever since Helen became famous, there
were those who believed that she was a fraud, and that
her accomplishments were really those of Anne Sullivan,
her teacher.

Helen passed the entrance exams with flying colors.
In the fall of 1900, she entered Radcliffe as a member of
the freshman class. Some people had suggested that she
would need more time to finish her degree, but she
refused to consider the idea. Helen wanted to prove that
she could carry the same workload as hearing and
sighted students.

The next four years were exhausting. Every day in
class, Anne sat beside her, spelling out every word of the
lecture in Helen's hand. Since Helen couldn't take notes
in class, she would jot them down in Braille afterwards,
depending largely on her memory.

Most of the books that she needed were not in Braille so Anne read to her for four or five hours a day, spelling out the text. Although surgery had somewhat restored her sight, Anne always had trouble with her eyes, and Helen felt terribly guilty that the strain of this kind of work was causing her vision to deteriorate even more.

Then in the middle of her second year, Helen agreed to write a book! She had been offered three thousand dollars for her autobiography, an extraordinary amount in those days. Still carrying a full course load, doing volunteer work for the deaf-blind, Helen completed the book in monthly installments for *The Ladies' Home Journal*. In March of 1903, *The Story of My Life* was published in book form. It was an instant critical success, and has been a classic ever since.

In 1904 Helen graduated from Radcliffe with honors. She had accomplished something that no other deaf-blind person had. For the rest of her life, she would champion the cause of blind and disabled people everywhere.